ZERO TO HERO IN UX DESIGN

A BEGINNER'S GUIDE TO CREATING ENGAGING USER EXPERIENCES

SAMBHAV SINGHVI

Made with ♥ on the Notion Press Platform
www.notionpress.com

Contents

Preface

Welcome to "Zero to Hero in UI/UX Design!" Get ready! You're about to journey from being a beginner to a design wizard. Soon, you'll get cozy with Figma. It doesn't matter if you've tried design before or if you're starting fresh (like, what even is a wireframe?). This book is made just for YOU! We won't just toss you fancy terms & call it good—oh no way! We're here to put everything down so it'll actually make sense (trust me!).

This book is your go-to starter pack for UI/UX design. We're diving into all sorts of fun topics—like wireframing & user flows—plus some super cool tricks too! We'll show you how to create awesome prototypes and learn those high-fidelity designs. If it feels like we're speaking some other language right now, don't sweat it! That's why this book is in your hands! By the end, you'll throw around design terms like a pro.

Honestly, the journey from zero to hero isn't a straight line—it's more like a squiggly worm on a breezy day. You might think, "What does this button do?" Guess what? That's totally normal! UX design isn't about being perfect; it's about learning, experimenting, & adjusting. It's all about giving users an amazing experience—even when they don't notice! We want smooth designs & functional vibes—not just pretty stuff that works as well as a chocolate teapot.

Get ready for real-life examples, handy tips, & shortcuts so you can avoid those rookie mistakes that many of us learned the hard way (yikes!). Think of this book as your digital buddy—a mentor guiding you through the chaos and showing that YES, YOU can turn wild ideas into sleek, usable designs!

So hang on tight! Because by the time you finish reading this book, you'll zoom from zero to full-on UI/UX hero. Ready to tackle client projects or create your own apps? Or maybe just show off how fancy your personal site looks? Let's dive in!

"Going from zero to hero in UI/UX? Strap in, because soon you'll be turning 'meh' designs into straight-up masterpieces."

CHAPTER ONE

INTRODUCTION TO UI & UX

What is UX ?

Okay, so UX (User Experience) is just about making sure that when you're using an app or website, it feels smooth and easy. It's like the magic happening behind the curtain so you don't get all mixed or ticked off. UX designers think a lot about how something works and feels—not just how it looks. Imagine using an app that's like gliding on ice vs. one that makes you wanna chuck your phone out the window!

A great UX means everything just... clicks! You know exactly where to tap, and how to uncover stuff, and nothing feels weird. Think about scrolling through TikTok or ordering from DoorDash—no big-brain workouts required! You just do it. That's some top-notch UX right there. But oh boy, let's talk about Bad UX! That's when buttons are hiding like they're playing hide-and-seek, the layout looks like a tornado hit, or it takes forever to load anything. Yikes! You might just bounce faster than a kid in a candy store!

And hey, it's not about cramming in flashy designs or cool features just to show off. No way! UX is all about figuring out what the user wants to do & making it stupid simple. Whether it's snagging some cool new shoes, watching funny cat videos, or finding that fire playlist, good UX makes sure there's zero struggle—only good vibes! You shouldn't feel like you have to go on a treasure hunt; it should flow like a lazy river on a hot day!

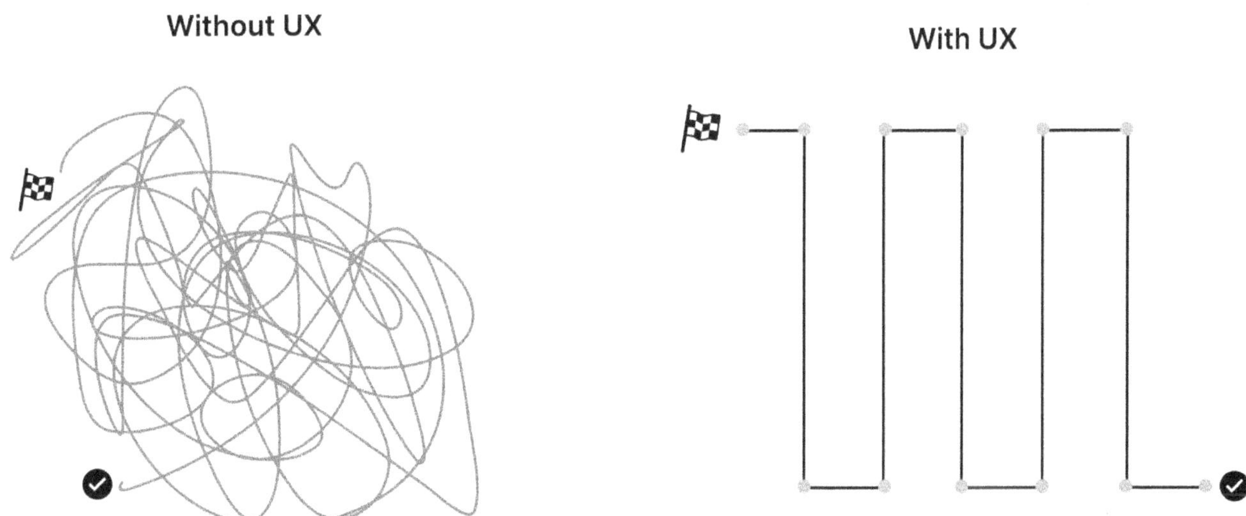

Importance of UX ?

Alright, buddy! Picture this: you've got a super cool app idea. But hey, the experience is a total flop, nobody's gonna stick around. That's where (User Experience) struts in—it's a complete game-changer! It's all about keeping users from feeling lost or totally bummed out while using your stuff. Get that vibe right, & folks will keep coming back; mess it up, they're PEACING OUT faster than you can say, "nope!"

First things first, UX is like the whole "first impression" gig. Have you ever clicked on a new app or website? If it's all janky and makes you scratch your head for more than 10 seconds, you're outta there—just like that! Good UX makes that first click feel as smooth as butter. It's kinda like showing up to a party where the tunes are awesome & the snacks are plentiful—you're gonna stick around! But if it feels awkward & you don't even know where the bathroom is? You're ghosting quicker than a friendly spirit.

Oh, and guess what? It's not just about looking flashy. Nope! UX actually plays a big role in how successful your product becomes. If folks can easily find what they want, snag something to buy, or sign up for stuff, they're more likely to hang out & do whatever you want them to do. But if they have to jump through fire hoops & walk on hot coals just to get started? Well...goodbye forever! So yeah, good UX makes it easy-peasy for users to get what they need—& that's gold for business.

In conclusion (or as I like to say: to wrap things up like a burrito), UX is really the secret sauce here. It's not just about having eye-catching designs; it's all about making the whole experience smooth, easy-peasy lemon squeezy, and just flat-out FUN! Nail that UX game, & people will totally vibe with your product—that's what you're aiming for!

"Good UX is like a joke—if you have to explain it, it's not that good"

Laws of UX (Boring but important)

Laws of UX are like secret cheat codes They help you make your designs super-du user-friendly. These are solid rules that keep the experience smooth, like butter! Let's break it down:

- **Hick Law:**
  More choices? More time to decide—like when you're at an ice cream shop! Keep it simple. Don't drown them in options.
- **Fitts's Law:**
  It's easier to click things if they're BIG & close., make your buttons nice and easy to hit. No one wants to play "find the button!"
- **Miller's Law:**
  People can only hold onto 7 pieces of info in their heads. It's like, too much info at once? Brain overload!
- **Jakob's Law:**
  Users expect your app to work like their fave apps. So, don't reinvent the wheel! Make it familiar so they don't feel lost.
- **The Aesthetic-Usability Effect:**
  If it looks good, folks think it works well—even if it doesn't do much! So yeah, keep it pretty and clean.

These laws help make sure users don't get lost or super frustrated—keeping things breezy & simple. Stick with these golden rules, and your designs will be totally awesome! You can find all the laws of UX on this website (https://lawsofux.com/)

Miller's Law

Jakob's Law

Psychology of UX

Alright, let's dive into the wild world of UX psychology! It's all getting inside folks' heads while they're using apps, websites, or anything digital. Imagine trying to figure out why someone would throw their phone out the window in frustration. UX designers want to keep users from rage quitting when things get too weird or annoying. They have a toolbox filled with psychological tricks to transform every interaction into smooth sailing. So, let's break it down nice:

Cognitive Load (aka brainwork)

This one's all about how much thinking you gotta do to figure things out. When an app or website is complicated, it feels like lifting weights with your brain! People don't wanna sit there scratching their heads looking for the "buy" button. Nope! They want a quick in-and-out experience. Good UX means lowering that cognitive load—making it super easy to use so you can breeze through without breaking a sweat.

Imagine scrolling through an app where everything is clear: buttons are shiny and beckoning, info is organized—everything fits together like puzzle pieces. That's what you want: low cognitive load, high happy vibes!

Attention Span (or lack of it)

Let's face it: our attention spans are shorter than a TikTok video! If an app doesn't grab us fast, people are outta there quicker than you can say "swipe left." UX design is all about keeping things quick and snappy. You gotta hook them instantly & make sure everything loads faster than a cat video on the internet. If things feel slow or look messy? Bye-bye!

The Power of Habits

We humans love our routines—like that one friend who orders the same thing at every restaurant. People expect new apps to work like the ones they already know. Social media apps all have that familiar layout, right? If your app makes users rethink everything they've learned about how apps should work, they'll get annoyed real quick. Stick to what's familiar so nobody feels like they're taking a surprise final exam.

Feedback Loops

When you do something on an app—like hitting "submit"—you expect some kind of response. Like when you send a text and hope for those little dots to pop up so you know it went through! This is called feedback in UX, and boy is it important! No feedback? Users think your app's toast or that aliens abducted their action! Total buzzkill!

Emotional Design

Alright, listen up! People are emotional beings—happy, sad, snacky... You get it! Good UX truly connects with these feelings. If an app feels fun or calming—bam! You got yourself a loyal user who loves hanging out on your platform. Apps like Instagram make using them feel like a walk in the park—light & breezy! But mess up that design? People will feel more stressed than before their morning coffee!

Choice Overload

Offering too many options can drive folks nuts—kinda like standing in front of 100 cereal boxes at the store and not knowing which one to pick! This fear of making decisions is called choice overload in UX—and it's real scary stuff. If users see too many buttons or options? They'll just stare blankly & give up altogether. Smart UX gives just enough choices so users can pick without feeling overwhelmed.

Flow State

Have you ever got lost in an app and suddenly realized it's been two hours? Welcome to flow state—the gold medal of UX design! It means everything clicks together so smoothly that users don't even notice time passing by—they're just cruising along having a good time without breaking rhythm!

Trust & Credibility

Trust is paramount in UX land! If your site looks sketchy (think creepy basement vibes), people will turn tail and run faster than during a fire drill. Good UX builds trust with neat designs & straightforward language—it says "Hey, we're safe here." When users feel secure with what you offer, they may stay longer—and maybe even bring cash!

So there ya go—the psychology game behind UX is all about figuring out how users think and feel while they interact with stuff. You want them to have an easy-breezy time without working too hard (or getting stressed). Designing for human brains means knowing what keeps folks engaged and what makes them want to book it!

"Design isn't just what it looks like or feels like—design is how it works." — Written by that Apple guy

What is UI ?

Now onto UI—it stands for User Interface—and it's what you see when using an app or website: buttons, icons, menus—you name it! Think of UI as the vibe check for any app; if it looks sharp & easy-peasy? You're sticking around; if it's messy or makes no sense? Nope!

Visuals and First Impressions

When you open your favorite app, the UI slaps you right in the face with layouts, colors & even animations! It's like meeting someone new—that first impression matters! Like scrolling through TikTok—all smooth and fun because its UI knows what it's doing.

Functionality and Flow

But hey, UI isn't just about looking pretty—it needs to function well too! The goal? Make sure that tapping buttons or filling forms feels as natural as breathing air (seriously!). Imagine if the "like" button on Instagram was hiding under a rock? Major buzzkill.

Consistency is Key

Good UI keeps things consistent; think of how most apps use familiar icons for stuff like settings or notifications—that saves folks from guesswork villainy! By sticking with common patterns, usability becomes smooth sailing.

Attention to Detail

UI loves details! Slick animations when swiping or buttons lighting up when tapped—it's those little touches that make things feel polished & satisfying.

Why UI Matters

To sum this up: UI is what we actually touch and see—but it's also more than just looks; it's all about creating experiences that feel seamless and kinda fun! When the UI rules? You hardly notice it—you're just enjoying yourself; when it's bad—oh boy—you're ready to peace out fast!

So remember: good design rocks—it keeps everyone coming back for more amazingness!

"UI is what you use, UX is how you feel using it"

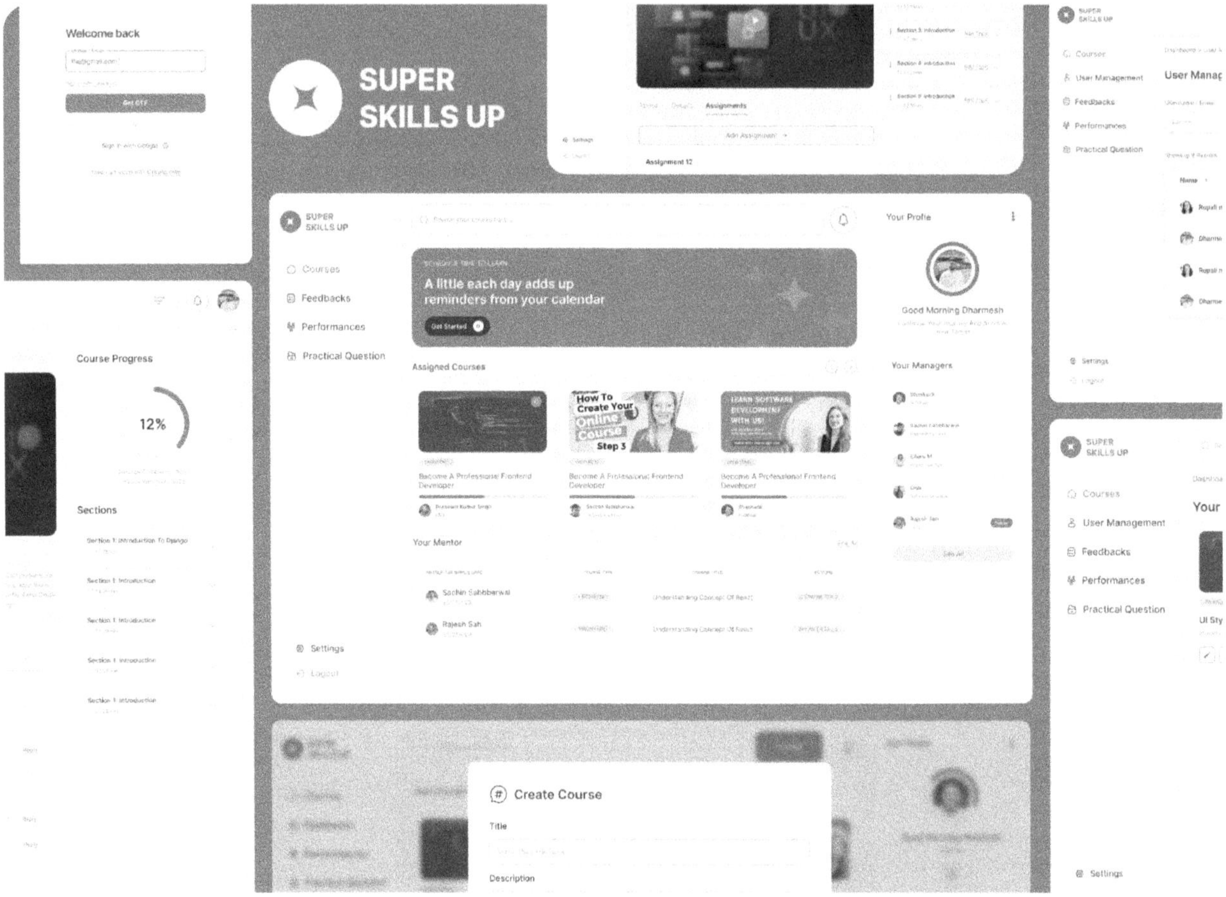

Home   About   Features

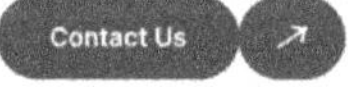

Sign In   **Sign Up**

Welcome to our exclusive Luxury Car Renting
Platform, where automotive excellence meets
discerning taste.

Contact Us

Is UI a part of UX ?

UI is definitely a part of UX, but they're not twins or! Picture UI as the "look" and "feel"—you know, the icons, & layouts that you poke at. On the other hand, UX is the entire journey of using the product.

Think it like this: UI is your snazzy outfit, while UX is how cozy & cool you feel strutting around in it. You can have a visually stunning UI—like a peacock showing off its feathers—but if the UX is terrible, it all goes downhill fast! They need to work together like peanut butter & jelly to ensure the app not only looks super fresh but also runs like a well-oiled machine.

Less Is More ?

In UI design, less is often more—kind of like a diet for screens! When you remove all that unnecessary clutter, users can actually focus on what matters. Imagine scrolling through an Instagram feed that's sleek and clean versus one jam-packed with ads and pop-ups; talk about a mood changer!

A simple, minimal design helps users do what they came for without losing their minds in a maze of distractions. The goal isn't to bombard them with options; it's about giving the right amount so they don't have to think too hard (which is great because thinking is hard!).

Simple design = smooth sailing experience!

"UI is what you use, UX is how you feel using it"

CHAPTER TWO

BEFORE YOU START ?

Who is this book for ?

This book is perfect for all the design noobs out there who want to level up their game show off some real skills in UI/UX. If you've been dreaming about creating smooth apps or websites that make users go "Wow!," but don't know how to, then this book is basically your new BFF. Whether you're a college kid exploring what to do with your life, a freelancer with some flavor to your portfolio, or even a developer who's fed up with clunky interfaces—this book's got your back.

Maybe you're an entrepreneur trying to make your app or site look super professional without emptying your wallet on a designer. Or perhaps you're just curious about design & want to whip up things that people can't get enough of. No matter where you're coming from, if you've got the hustle but lack the know-how, this book will help transform you from a total UI/UX rookie into a design superstar!

We're talking straightforward steps, useful tips from the real world, and guidance that won't leave you scratching your head like you just finished a boring textbook. Seriously, this is the glow-up your design skills have been waiting for!

Main goal of this book ?

Ready to go from "Who even is a designer?" to "Look at my stunning creations!"? Our main goal is simple: help you boost your design skills without drowning in boring lectures & big words. Seriously, we want you to have fun while learning how to make awesome, user-friendly designs that don't just look cool but actually work well.

Are you dreaming of designing sleek websites or apps that people can't stop clicking? Maybe you just wanna figure out how to create stuff people enjoy using. Either way, this book is on a mission! We want you to awaken your inner design superstar. By the end of these pages, you'll understand everything—even the fancy terms like layouts and typography! And yes, we'll also throw in some juicy tidbits on user flows and prototypes.

Feeling excited yet? Good! We're here to make sure you feel pumped up—not stuck in a design mess. The vibe of this book is all about being chill and practical. We're ditching the fluff & the head-scratching theory for real skills that'll get you designing faster than you can say "What's a wireframe?"

When you're finished, you won't just know what UI/UX means; you'll know how to use it like a pro! Get ready for a design glow-up from zero to hero. Time to show off those skills—you got this!

"Shoot for the moon. Even if you miss, you'll land among the Wi-Fi signals."

CHAPTER THREE

Let's start with a bang ?

Terms & concepts

Let's dive into some important terms in UI/UX design. Don't worry, I will keep it easy and fun1.

Wireframe :

Think of a wireframe as the skeleton of your design. It's pretty much like drawing a rough outline of where everything goes on your app or website. Buttons, images, text blocks—everything has its place. It's simple stuff, usually black & white—no fancy colors yet! Just remember it's like sketching before you paint the masterpiece.

Prototype :

Now, a prototype is the cool upgrade from a wireframe. It's like trying out a pizza before you buy it (yummy!). You can actually click buttons, scroll around, and see how it feels in real life! It's that moment of 'does this outfit look good on me?' before you yell 'I'll take it!'

User Flow :

User flow is all about the journey of a user doing something fun—like ordering pizza through an app. First, you open that delightful app. Next, search for yummy restaurants, pick your pizza, customize your order, and pay up! A smooth user flow is like GPS for your app—no getting lost here!

Call to Action (CTA) :

Ever seen a button shouting "Hey YOU! Click me!"? That's a call to action! It's what pushes users to do stuff like "Buy Now," "Sign Up," or "Subscribe." A good CTA is like having your own cheerleader guiding you to the next step!

Accessibility :

This is all about making sure everyone can enjoy your app or website—even your pals with disabilities! Imagine throwing a party where everyone is invited! This means using easy-to-read fonts, bright colors that pop, screen readers for those who need them, and navigation that even a goldfish could manage.

Information Architecture (IA) :

IA is how all your content and features are organized on your site or app—like having a tidy closet so you don't lose your favorite socks! If it's well done, finding what you need feels like a walk in the park instead of searching for treasure maps that don't exist.

Responsive Design :

Responsive design makes sure your website looks awesome on any device. Laptop? Check! Phone? You got it! Tablet? Absolutely! The layout adjusts so you won't find yourself zooming in and scrolling sideways like it's the early 2000s!

Usability Testing :

Oh boy, usability testing is when you let real users try out your design while you sit back and grab some popcorn! Watch what goes well and what totally flops—kind of like letting someone else play with your favorite game until they hit a surprise level they weren't ready for!

So there you have it! Easy peasy terms in UI/UX design without melting your brain!

"Wireframing is like building the foundation of a house—without it, your design might look good but won't stand strong."

Let's introduce you to "My Design process"

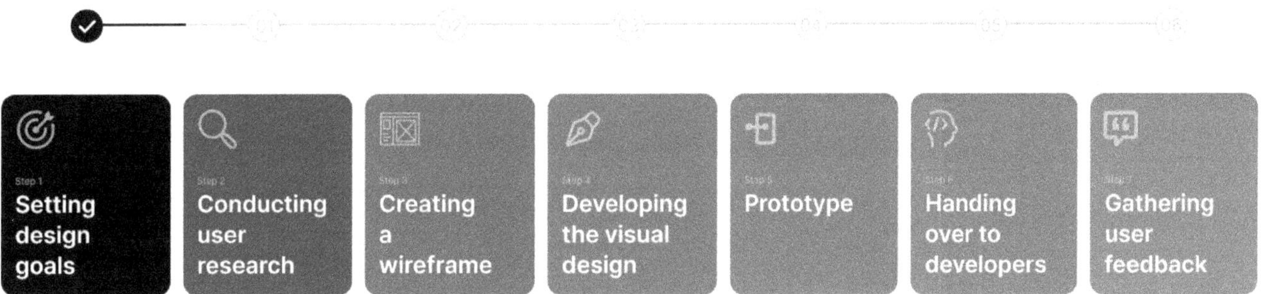

Let's dive into UI design like a kid jumps into a pile of leaves What's the fun in this Here's how the whole adventure goes down:

Setting Design Goals

First, we've got to figure out what we're aiming for—like between pizza or tacos for dinner. Seriously, before you even think about how things will look ask yourself: What's the end? This goal-setting is all about laying the. You want to know why you're designing it and what problem you're tackling for users. Think about what they want, what the business says it needs, and how you'll know when you've hit the jackpot! For instance, if you're making an online shopping app, you might want to make sure people can check out faster than a hungry cheetah. Clear goals are like a GPS: they help you not get lost along the way.

Conducting User Research

Now comes the detective work! User research is where you get your spyglass and try to peek into users' minds (without being creepy). It's all about finding out what makes them tick—what drives them bananas and what they really need. Use surveys, interviews, or even old data. The aim? Get deep into their brains! What excites them? What bugs them? It's like becoming their best buddy so you can create something that actually helps! Skip this step, and you might be playing a game with no rules!

Creating a Wireframe

So, you've got your goals and your users—now it's sketch time! Wireframing is like doodling your dream house before picking out paint colors or that funky couch. Here, you lay out the basic design structure without worrying about looking fancy yet. We're talking about where buttons go and where text squishes fit in! Wireframes are simple blueprints guiding how users will wander through your digital wonderland before any pizzazz gets added.

Developing the Visual Design

With a solid wireframe down, let's jazz it up! Visual design is where it gets fun—like decorating your room after you've moved in. Choose colors, fonts, and icons that scream "cool"! It's more than just making things pretty; it's about leading users' eyes to what's important—kind of like a sign pointing to free cookies. A fabulous design feels fresh but also makes sure everything works smoothly for the user. This part is what transforms your app from "meh" to "wow!"

Prototype

Now that you're eye-popping with visuals, it's prototype time! Think of a prototype as trying on shoes before buying them—it lets users play around a bit! They can click buttons and saunter through screens without everything being perfect yet (which is kind of like spaghetti night at home!). The aim? Observe how they navigate through this test run: smoothly gliding or dodging bumps? Catch any oopsies now before diving deep into development because fixing things then is like trying to change a tire while driving.

Handing Over to Developers

After your masterpiece is ready (well, almost), it's time for some teamwork magic with developers! You don't just send the design off and say "good luck!" Nope! You work together closely to ensure they know exactly how awesome you want this product to be. You'll give them tools—like style guides or image assets—to turn those dreams into reality! Keep talking throughout because sometimes tech hurdles pop up that might mean adjustments are needed—like suddenly realizing there won't be enough room for that giant unicorn statue in your backyard!

Gathering User Feedback

Finally, once everything's up and running, guess what? The journey continues! Gathering feedback is like asking friends if they liked your cookie recipe post on social media (hopefully they did!). Listen to users crying for help or cheering for joy over specific features. Do surveys or study their behaviors using cool analytics tools (which sound fancy but are really just numbers telling stories). The goal here is to make sense of how it all works in real life. By using their thoughts, you'll keep refining the experience and stay in tune with what they love.

So there you have it! The UI design process takes you from crystal-clear goals straight through prototype testing—all while ensuring users are happy explorers in this digital land of wonder where great designs flourish and work like magic!

Gathering requirements

Gathering UX requirements is like figuring out what snacks to bring on a movie night. wanna know what your audience craves when you start the show! No one enjoys a boring movie, right? So, don't just guess. It's time to poke around in the minds of your users. You gotta find out what they really wanna use.

First thing's first: **chat with your users**. You can't just assume you know their favorite flavor of ice cream based on your own cravings. Slide into their DMs with surveys or chat over coffee (or hot cocoa if it's chilly). Ask them what annoys them and how they wrestle with similar apps or websites. Get the juicy details straight from the source. It's like gossip, but for tech!

Now, let's talk about **user personas**—these are like imaginary friends for your project. Build profiles that show who your users are. Think about age, job, hobbies (did I mention pizza?). These personas keep you grounded when you face design dilemmas. When you're stuck, just ask yourself, "What would our persona do?" Simple, right?

Next up, **snatch a peek at the competition**. Spy on apps or sites that are kinda like yours. What are they nailing? Where are they tripping? Jot down notes on both sides of the coin. This helps you see what users want & how to make their experience sparkle!

Don't forget about **stakeholders!** They're like the bosses at your video game—funders and marketing folks who need their goals met too. It can feel a bit like juggling flaming torches—don't drop any! Keep everyone satisfied while aiming for a product that doesn't flop.

Analytics data is another goodie. If you've got an app or site already running, peek at how users behave—where do they bounce off like rubber balls? Which pages get all their clicks? It's sort of like low-key spying on their habits (totally for good reasons). This helps you spot trouble areas that scream confusion.

Lastly, don't skip user **testing early in the game.** You can whip up some rough sketches or simple prototypes and let a few brave souls give them a whirl. Watching folks interact with your design is kinda like testing your favorite party playlist—does it make people dance or hide in a corner? Spot those hiccups early so you can fix them before going too far down the rabbit hole.

When all's **said & done**, you'll have an awesome list of must-haves, nice-to-haves, & things to avoid like the plague. These requirements will steer your design process & make sure your finished masterpiece resonates with users while still keeping those higher-ups grinning!

Strategy to start with your design

Kicking off a UI/UX design project for a client? Oh boy, it can be super exciting but also kinda tricky! Here's a fun & simple way to cover all the important steps. This way, you'll deliver a design that blows their socks off:

Get Vibe Check:

First, you gotta know what the client is all about. into their brand, who they want to reach, & what they hope to achieve with this project. Don't forget to snag all the juicy details in a client brief! Also, take a peek at their competitors—what's the vibe out there?

Set the Scene:

Now it's time to kick things off! Organize a fun kickoff meeting to get everyone on the same page about goals & what you'll deliver. Set clear goals! Make sure you have some success metrics too—gotta know if you're winning, right?
     Next up, whip up a timeline. Throw in key milestones so you don't go off the rails!

Wireframe Wonderland:

Let's create some basic wireframes. These babies show where everything will fit in your design! Once done, share 'em with the client for some early feedback. This is where changes can save your bacon!

Design Like a Boss:

Now it's time to shine! Make high-fidelity mockups with fancy stuff like colors, fonts, & pictures galore. Your design should totally match the client's brand—no way they want to look mismatched!

Prototype Power:

Get your hands dirty (not literally!) and build an interactive prototype. Show how your design will work! Make sure it shows user flows & key interactions. Then, get ready for the big reveal.

Feedback Frenzy:

Time to strut your stuff! Present that prototype to your client & soak up their feedback like a sponge. Tweak things based on what they say—refine that design until it sparkles!

Test & Iterate:

Usability testing comes next! See how real users handle your design. Are they confused or impressed? Use their feedback to make it even better.

Launch Like a Pro:

Wowza, we're almost there! Finalize everything and team up with developers for launch prep. Keep an eye on things during launch day—all hands on deck for smooth sailing!

Post-Launch Love:

Once launched, keep watching how it performs.

Collecting feedback from users and the client will help too! Offer ongoing support and check in often—everyone likes a little love after launch.

There you go! Follow these steps for an awesome design journey that impresses your client and makes users say "Wow!" Who knew design could be this much fun?

"Step one of every project: Panic. Step two: Pretend to know what you're doing. Step three: Design something awesome."

Competitive analysis (Taking inspo is important)

Checking out the competition is kinda like stalking—just, you know, the business version! You look at what others are doing. Peek at their designs, see what works, & ask yourself, "What's missing here?"

Now listen up! This isn't about straight-up copying folks. Nope! It's more like taking a little inspiration from the cool stuff around. It's a treasure hunt for trends & gaps! You want to whip up something that'll make people say, "Wow!"

Also, don't forget to snoop through user reviews. They're like gold mines for what people dig or totally despise. This gives you an edge in creating your own design that pops like a firecracker. So dive into that competitive pool. Get some ideas! Mix 'em up with your own flavor to craft the best design ever! Go on, get creative!

Don't fear to ask more questions to client

Alright, let's break this down: don't be shy about bombarding your client with questions. Seriously! Asking lots of questions isn't a hint that you're clueless. Nope! It's all about getting the juicy details so you can serve up something amazing.

Imagine it like texting before hanging out, right? You just want to make sure you're both the same. If you skip them, you might stroll in and realize you've got the complete wrong vibe. Oops! The same thing goes for design work—you don't wanna start whipping up something when you only have a fuzzy idea in your head.

Clarity is key, folks! The more curious you are, the better you can shape your project to their actual needs. Not just what you THINK they want. Plus, clients really dig it when you ask more questions—it shows you're invested in getting it spot-on!

So, let those questions fly! Ask away—even if it feels repetitive or dive deep into details that seem a tad ridiculous. Trust me; it'll save you way more headaches later on. You'll end up looking like a total pro when the project goes off without a hitch the first time around. High five to that!

CHAPTER FOUR

TOOLS YOU NEED AS A BEGINNER ?

Figma is all you need.

Okay, let's break it down. When people say, "Figma is all you need," they're basically claiming Figma is the best—like a superhero of design tools! It's like having a Swiss Army knife but for folks who do UI and UX stuff. Want to sketch wireframes? Done! Need to whip up some fancy designs? You got it! Or maybe you're prototyping? Figma totally got your back!

Now, here's the kicker. It's all in the cloud! So you & your friends can work together right then & there. No more waiting to send files back & forth like it's some kind of old-school email game. Just share a link, and voilà—everyone's on the same page (literally, no jokes here).

But wait, there's more! Figma is super flexible. Whether you're crafting a website or a mobile app or just having fun with ideas, it's got everything in one spot. No need to hop around from one app to another like a confused rabbit—Figma is that one-stop shop! It's neat, quick, & keeps your projects nice and tidy. So if you're using Figma? You're totally winning!

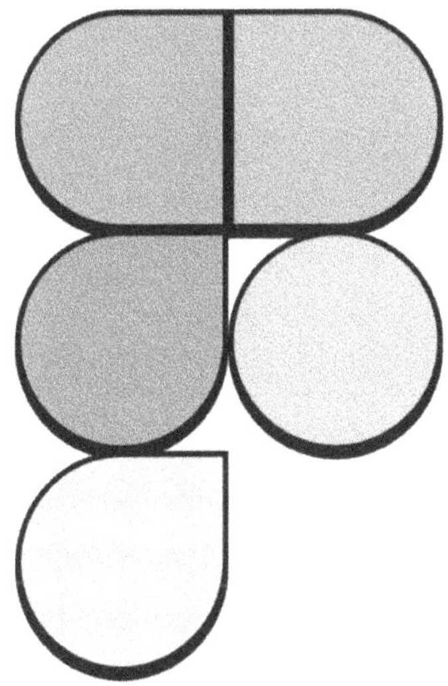

The best way to learn figma?

Alright, if you're trying to level up your Figma game, YouTube is your secret weapon. For real, the best way to learn is to dive into those tutorials and start building along with them. It's like getting free lessons from pros who already figured out all the hacks and shortcuts.

Just search for design tutorials, and you'll find everything from beginner stuff to advanced tricks. The cool part? You can pause, rewind, and follow along at your own pace—no pressure. YouTube's basically the design school that doesn't charge tuition, and you can pick up tips while chilling in bed.

The more you work through tutorials, the faster you'll get comfortable with Figma's tools. Before you know it, you'll be whipping up designs like a pro, all from binge-watching a few vids. It's like Netflix, but instead of a new show, you're walking away with some serious skills.

CHAPTER FIVE

KICK START WITH A PLAN

Knowing your user (User persona)

Let's dig right in!

"Knowing your user" is kind of like figuring out who you're designing for, but on a way deeper level. It's not about throwing spaghetti at the wall to see what sticks. I know how sometimes you think, "What do I post to get likes from my followers?" Well, in UI/UX, you flip that script. Your followers? They're users! Instead of likes, you want smooth experiences. (Yes, smoother than my last cup of coffee!)

Now, let's talk about user personas. Think of it as crafting a super detailed character profile of your ideal user. It goes beyond their age or job or even where they hang their hat—this is about diving into their goals, frustrations & behaviors. What makes them tick? Picture this: You're designing an app for students. Your persona might look something like this:

- Name: Jess, 21
- Job: College student
- Needs: Fast access to notes & easy study
- Tools Frustrations : Complicated interfaces (ugh!), slow-loading
- Pages Goals : Zoom through studying so she can do... Well, anything else!

You kinda create a mini-movie script for this "character." This way, when you design, you really picture who you're designing for—no more guessing like it's some sort of game show.

Now, why do we care? Because if you don't get your users, then guess what? You will end up designing for yourself or whatever YOU think they want! Talk about a risky move! You might slap on some fancy features that seem awesome but totally miss the boat. When do you actually know your user? It's like having a secret cheat code—you design with purpose, fixing real-life problems instead of just adding stuff because it looks good.

So imagine you're cooking up a fitness app. If your persona is "Mike—a busy dad at 35 who needs quick workouts," then boom! You focus on a straightforward app with speedy routines. But if your persona is "Sarah—a 22-year-old fitness fan who can't get enough stats," then it's time to build serious features for tracking her fitness journey.

The goal is simple: Knowing your user means every little design choice helps tackle their problems and makes their life super easy-peasy! Think of it like creating a playlist—if you don't know what jams they love, then good luck picking the right tracks (or designs). Happy designing!

Journey Map

Okay, let's dive into it! So, a Journey Map is kinda like creating a treasure map but for users instead of pirates searching for gold. You plot everything out—from the first step they take until they reach the treasure at the end. It's just like planning a fun road trip! You know, you've got to figure out all the cool stops, those nasty traffic jams that ruin your vibe, and where to snag some grub (because who can travel on an empty stomach?).

Now think about this with your app or website. You map their journey! Like how they first discover your amazing product (maybe through an ad on social media that made them chuckle), what they do next, how they feel during the ride, and if they hit any bumps along the way—like trying to fit a square peg in a round hole. It's seeing things from their viewpoint so you can catch those epic highs and those "oh no" lows.

Picture this: you're crafting an online store. Your Journey Map would trace how someone lands on your site (scouring Facebook for cat memes or something), checks out the goods, tosses items into their cart like they're playing Tetris, & finally reaches the checkout stage. All while keeping tabs on their joyride—are they ecstatic because everything looks slick and prices are awesome? Or are they fuming because the checkout process resembles trying to solve a Rubik's Cube?

The whole goal here is smooth sailing—no bumps! You want their adventure to be super chill from that very first click to when they get that sweet confirmation screen saying "yay, you did it!" If there's any tricky spot—like a form that looks like it was designed by a toddler or a loading time so long it makes watching paint dry seem exciting—you wanna fix that before they bail faster than someone escaping a bad date.

In a nutshell, a Journey Map is your secret weapon in understanding precisely how users dance through your product. Where do they stumble? Where do they shine? You aim to make everything seamless—like planning the perfect road trip so nobody ends up lost wandering off into the wilderness!

Example

Persona:

- **Name:** Emma
- **Age:** 27
- **Job:** Marketing manager
- **Goal:** Snag a fabulous outfit for an upcoming event

1. Discovery Stage

- Step : So, Emma spots an Instagram ad for your store.
- Feeling: She's intrigued but kinda on guard.
- Touchpoint: Social media.
- Pain point: Doubts if the store actually has what she's dreaming of.

2. Exploration Stage

- Step : She clicks the ad like it's a golden ticket and lands on your homepage.

- Feeling : All kinds of curious & hopeful!
- Touchpoint : The homepage and all those product listing pages.
- Pain point : Total overload from too many options or categories that look like a maze!

3. Consideration Stage

- Step : She's browsing through all those delightful dresses.
- Feeling : Excited but also, more options, please!
- Touchpoint : Product pages (with images, details, & reviews).
- Pain point : If the descriptions are vague or the pictures look like potato photos, she might huff & leave in frustration.

4. Decision Stage

- Step : Emma adds a dress to her cart like it's a trophy!
- Feeling : Confident about her choice but suddenly questioning if she can afford fancy takeout next week.
- Touchpoint : Shopping cart vibes.
- Pain point : Yikes! If shipping costs shoot up or the checkout is as tangled as a spaghetti junction, she could bail.

5. Checkout Stage

- Step : She carries on to checkout, types her info in like she's signing her life away, and finally places the order!
- Feeling : A wee bit anxious about payment—will her wallet cry? Is the delivery squirrel fast enough?
- Touchpoint : The thrilling checkout process.
- Pain point : If the forms are longer than her last date's excuses or return policies make her head spin, she might just close her laptop in despair.

6. Post-Purchase Stage

- Step : Emma gets a confirmation email and delivery updates (cue relief!).
- Feeling : A mix of joy & eager anticipation for when her package arrives!
- Touchpoint : Good ol' email love.
- Pain point : But wait… if there's a delay or they ghost her on updates, anxiety might creep back in and maybe some regret too.

Insights:

At each stage, we catch a glimpse of Emma's feelings & possible hiccups along the way (like lovely speed bumps). If your checkout feels like solving a Rubik's Cube blindfolded, she won't stick around to play shop anymore! Mapping out this journey helps ensure every touchpoint is as smooth as butter— from curiosity to delivery excitement—making sure she walks away with not just the dress but a grin!

In conclusion, this journey map peeks into Emma's emotional rollercoaster and helps fix any bumps that could stop her from giving you her money again (because let's be honest—we want this gal coming back for round two!). It's all about turning first-time shoppers into loyal fans with zero hassles along the way—now that sounds like winning!

Make a User flow. Wait, what is user flow ?

A User Flow is like a treasure map for your users. It shows the exact steps they take to reach their goal on your website or app. Think of it as their journey, with every pitstop noted. Whether they're signing up for super cool, buying that awesome gadget, or just window shopping—user flow catches all the fun interactions along the way.

Alright, let's have some examples! Picture this: You're creating a food delivery app. The user flow for someone trying to place an order might look like this:

1. Opening the app (hopefully not too slow!).
2. Scrolling through restaurants (so many choices!).
3. Choosing a yum meal.
4. Tossing it into the cart (like adding cookies to your grocery list).
5. Filling out those delivery details (don't forget the address!).
6. Paying & confirming the order (the most serious step!).

This flow is all about how a user strolls from point A to point B, with plenty of stops along the way. It's like playing a video game – each choice takes them one step closer to victory until they reach that delicious prize.

But wait—here's the kicker: a user flow shows where things might go hilariously wrong. Are people getting stuck in some weird maze? Or are they vanishing like socks in a dryer? That's your cue to tweak things! You want your users to glide through it like butter on hot toast, not wrestling with the app like it's a rogue alligator.

So to sum it up: user flow is really about making sure the path your users take is smooth & clear, getting them across the finish line without having them throw down their phones in frustration. Because nobody wants to rage-quit their food delivery just because they got lost!

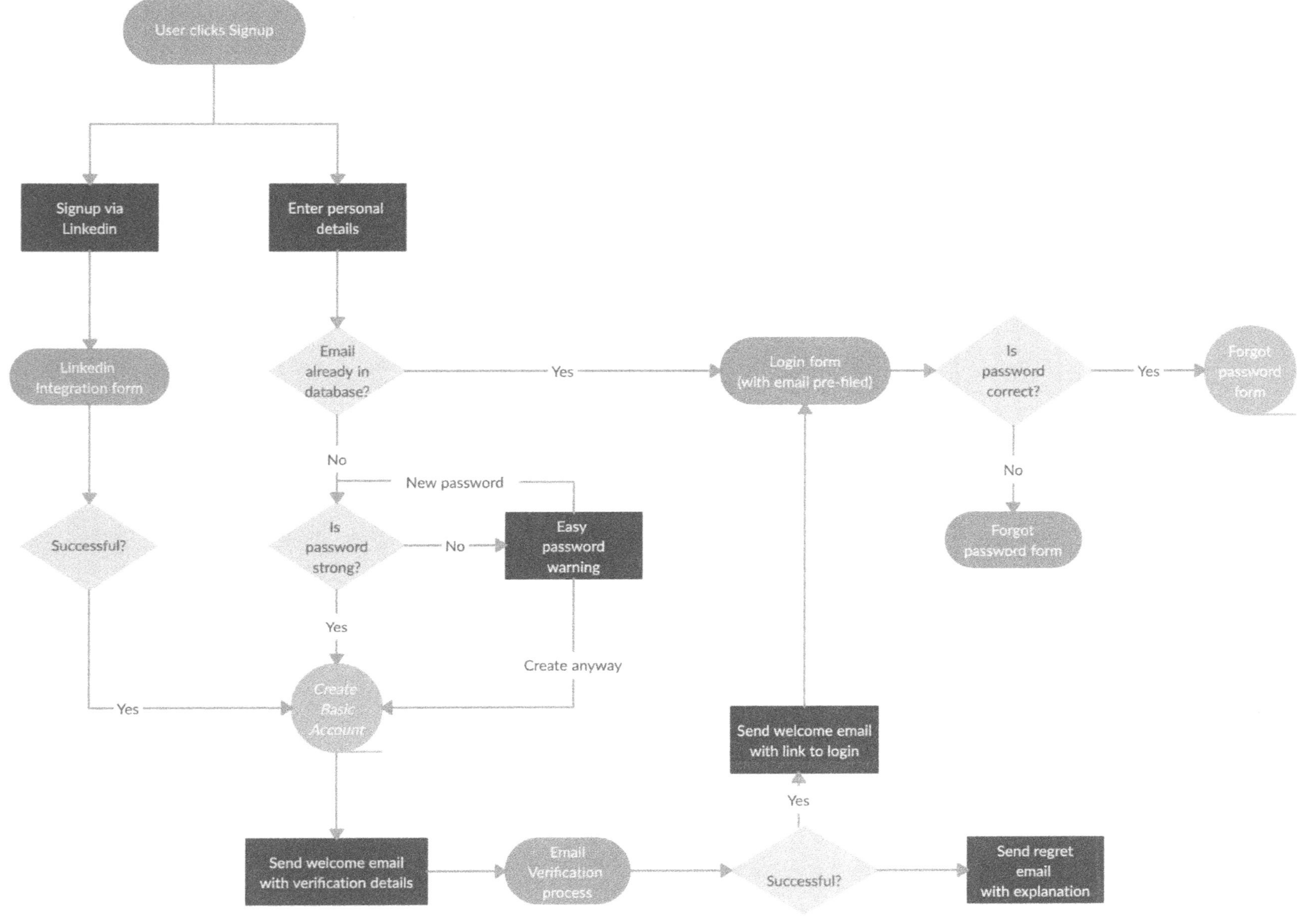

User clicks Signup
Signup via Linkedin
Enter personal details
Linkedin Integration form
Email already in database?
Yes
Login form (with email pre-filled)
Is password correct?
Yes
Forgot password form
No
Successful?
No
Is password strong?
No
Easy password warning
New password
Forgot password form
Yes
Yes
Create anyway
Create Basic Account
Send welcome email with link to login
Yes
Send welcome email with verification details
Email Verification process
Successful?
Send regret email with explanation
Yes

Information Architecture

Information Architecture (IA) is basically how you organize and structure all the content on a website or app, so people can actually find what they're looking for without getting lost. Think of it like the skeleton of your design—it holds everything together and makes sure stuff is in the right place.

Imagine you walk into a grocery store, but there's no signage, and everything is randomly placed. You'd be wandering around for ages trying to find a simple thing like milk, right? That's what a website or app would feel like without proper IA. You need to have clear categories, logical menus, and easy-to-follow paths so users can find stuff fast without feeling like they're lost in a maze.

When you're building IA, you're thinking about how to group related content, how to label things so they make sense to users, and how to make the navigation smooth. It's all about making sure the user doesn't have to think too hard to find what they want. You've got to get inside their heads and ask: "What's the most logical place they'd look for this info?"

For example, if you're designing an e-commerce site, your IA would include stuff like categories for products (clothing, electronics, home goods), filters (size, price, color), and an easy-to-use search bar. You wouldn't want shoes mixed in with kitchen appliances, right? It's all about grouping content in a way that feels natural to the user.

At the end of the day, good IA means your users can quickly and effortlessly navigate through your site or app without feeling confused. It's like laying down road signs so no one gets lost on the way to their destination.

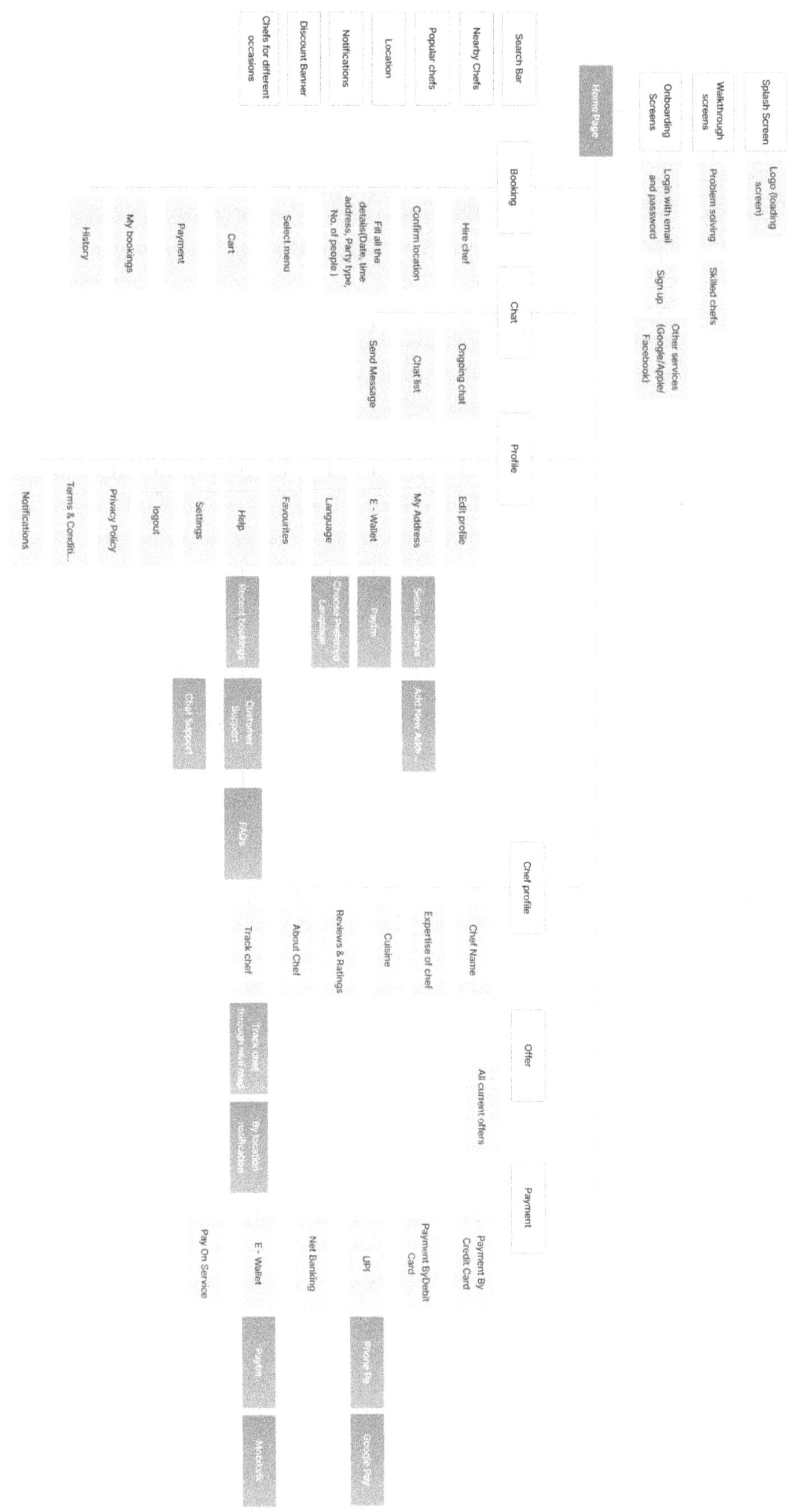

Splash Screen
Logo (loading screen)
Walkthrough screens
Problem solving
Skilled chefs
Onboarding Screens
Login with email and password
Sign up
Other services (Google/Apple/Facebook)
Home Page
Search Bar
Nearby Chefs
Popular chefs
Location
Notifications
Discount Banner
Chefs for different occasions
Booking
Hire chef
Confirm location
Fill all the details(Date, time, address, Party type, No. of people)
Select menu
Cart
Payment
My bookings
History
Chat
Ongoing chat
Chat list
Send Message
Profile
Edit profile
My Address
Select Address
Add New Add..
E - Wallet
Paytm
Language
Choose Preferred Language
Favourites
Help
Customer Support
Chef Support
FAQs
Settings
logout
Privacy Policy
Terms & Condtii...
Notifications
Recent bookings
Chef profile
Chef Name
Expertise of chef
Cuisine
Reviews & Ratings
About Chef
Track chef
Track chef through next meal
By location notification
Offer
All current offers
Payment
Payment By Credit Card
Payment By Debit Card
UPI
Phone Pe
Google Pay
Net Banking
E - Wallet
Paytm
Mobikwik
Pay On Service

CHAPTER SIX

JUMPING INTO DESIGN

Getting your hands dirty with Wireframing

Wireframing! It's like the very first step in crafting a website or app. Picture it as sketching out how everything fits together—without fretting over the fancy details. Kind of like drawing a stick figure instead of a full-on masterpiece. You're just figuring out where all the stuff goes: buttons, text, pictures—everything—before you slap on the icing.

You know when you're rearranging your bedroom? First, you choose where the bed, desk, and closet hang out before you get wild with posters and stuffed animals? Yup! That's what wireframing does for design. You're putting your "furniture" (think menus and buttons) in all the right spots so it looks neat & tidy.

Right now, this isn't about glamorous design. Nope! Just simple boxes and placeholders. You want to make sure everything's not hidden under piles of clutter—because we don't want users feeling lost like they wandered into a maze. Focus on function over all that flair!

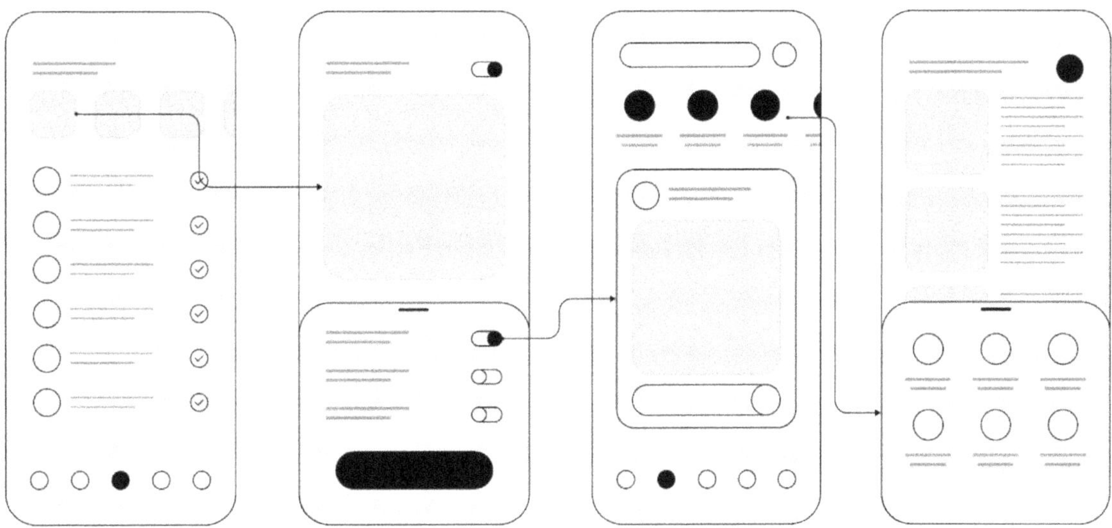

Why Wireframing Matters:

- **Laying Out the Vibes:** You're getting the overall structure down—making sure the homepage, product pages, or profiles all make sense. It's like mapping out the flow before you dive into the details.
- **User Flow on Point:** You're figuring out how people will actually use the app or site. You want the layout to make sense for users, so they're not clicking around clueless. Think of it like making sure they know exactly how to get from A to B without getting lost.
- **No Need for the Aesthetics Yet:** This is the chill stage. You're not worrying about colors, fonts, or images right now. It's all black and white, basic as can be. You don't need it to look Insta-worthy yet—just functional.
- **Quick Fixes and Feedback:** Wireframing makes it easy to experiment and get feedback. Like, if someone doesn't like how the nav bar or buttons are placed, you can quickly shuffle things around without spending hours perfecting it. Saves time and energy.
- **Faster Design Game:** Wireframes help you avoid going deep into full-on design only to realize later that something's off. You catch problems early, fix them, and then start adding all the style and visuals when everything is already on point

Imagine This:

You're designing a food delivery app. In the wireframe, you'd have simple squares for food items, rectangles for buttons like "Add to Cart," and maybe a basic bar at the top for search. No colors, no photos—just barebones, like doodling the layout. It's all about the flow and making sure everything's in the right spot.

You'd create a few versions, see what works, and then move on to the actual design later. At this stage, you're focused on making sure the app is easy to navigate and users can get what they want without bouncing. You're building the foundation first, so when you start adding the real design, everything feels tight and flows smoothly.

Low-fi vs. High-fi:

Low-fidelity wireframes:

These are super basic sketches, either on paper or with tools like Figma. They're all boxes and lines—nothing fancy, just pure function.

High-fidelity wireframes:

These are more detailed, with maybe a few more design elements thrown in but still not the final look. You're slowly getting closer to how the site or app will actually work and look.

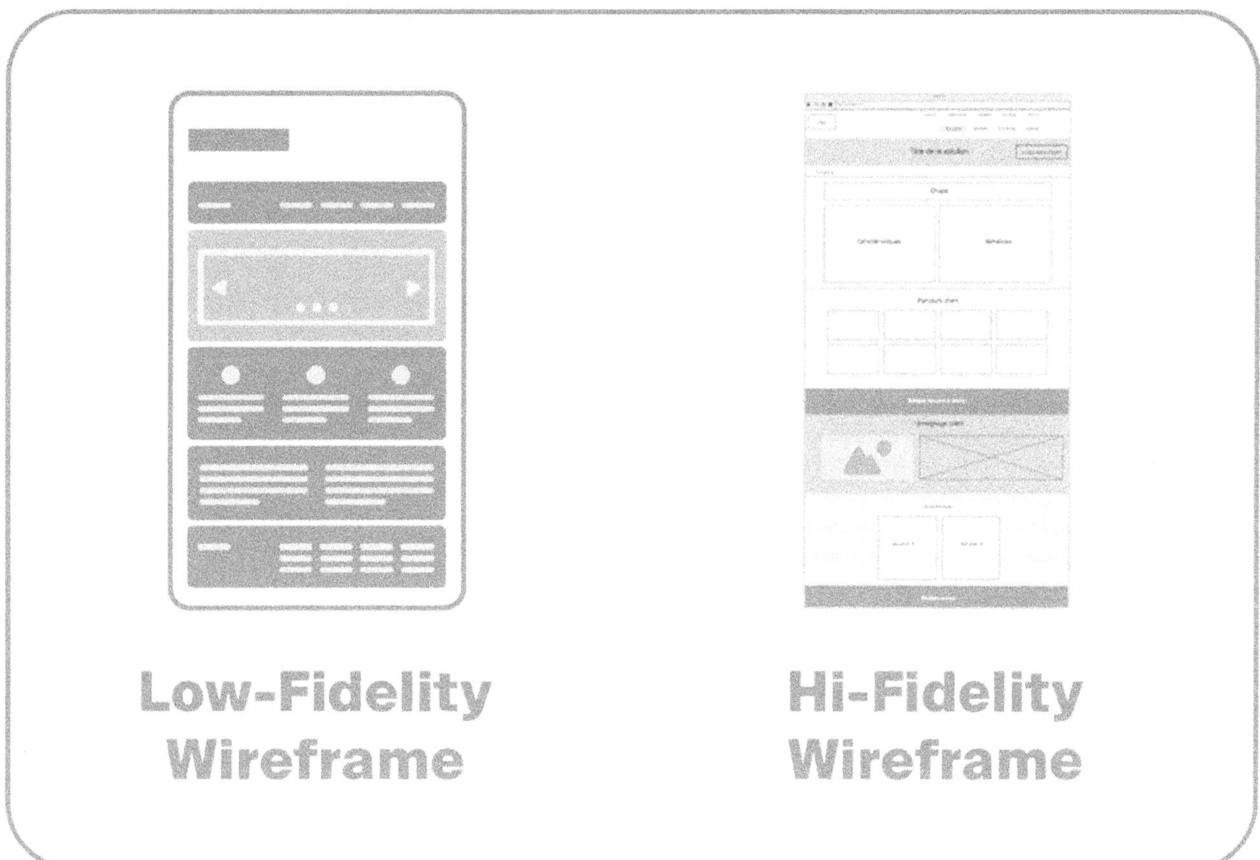

In short, wireframing is like putting together the blueprint before you go all-in on the final product. It's not about being pretty—it's about making sure everything's in the right place, works smoothly, and sets the vibe for what's coming next. Once that's locked in, you can start flexing your design skills.

UX guidelines for Mobile & Web design

Alright, let's talk about UX guidelines for mobile & web design. Think of them as the golden rules for making your app or website user-friendly. You want it to look sharp, be easy to use, and absolutely avoid anything that'd make users throw their phones out the window. Seriously, no one wants a design that acts like a puzzle—save that for your Sunday crossword!

Here's what you need to know:

- **Keep it Simple**
  Nobody has time for designs that make them scratch their heads. Whether it's a tiny phone or a big laptop screen, aim for clean & easily navigable. Users should be able to find where to click without needing a treasure map! Like I said, they want to get stuff done—not solve mysteries.
- **Touch Targets on Mobile**
  Imagine trying to tap something on your phone with big thumbs. Make those buttons generous in size—you want taps, not misses! Nobody likes playing darts with tiny buttons—trust me on this.
- **Responsive Design**
  This is a major deal! Your design has to look good on any screen size. It's like making sure you look decent from every angle—even if you're wearing pajamas at home (some of us are experts at that!). You don't want a squished or stretched layout when people switch devices.
- **Fast Loading Times**
  Speed is king! If your app or site takes ages to load, poof! Users are gone like magic. Especially on mobile; they're always in a hurry! Optimize those images & code so everything loads quickly as a flash.
- **Keep Navigation Easy**
  Your navigation bar? It should be as clear as day! Users should instantly know where they need to go. On mobile, think about that classic hamburger menu (the three lines). It keeps everything neat until users are hungry for more!
- **Consistent Design**
  Don't go switching styles like it's fashion week every other page! Keep colors, fonts, and buttons steady throughout so users don't get lost. It'd be super weird if someone changed outfits mid-conversation—so keep it consistent!
- **Accessibility**
  This is HUGE! Everyone should be able to navigate your design comfortably—including folks with disabilities. Use readable fonts and ensure enough contrast between text and background! Make it easy for everyone—like sending out invites to a fun party.
- **Minimize Pop-ups**
  Pop-ups can drive anyone crazy—especially when you're using your phone! No one wants their screen blocked by random ads popping up every few seconds. It's like having someone interrupt you mid-sentence—it's just rude!
- **Easy Forms**
  When it comes to forms (sign-ups, checkouts), keep them super simple and friendly! Use auto-fill whenever possible & keep fields at a minimum. Long forms? Total turn-offs—especially on
  mobile where typing feels like a workout.
- **Use Visual Feedback**
  When it comes to forms (sign-ups, checkouts), keep them super simple and friendly! Use auto-fill whenever possible & keep fields at a minimum. Long forms? Total turn-offs—especially on mobile where typing feels like a workout.

- **Test, Test, Test**
  Last but not least—always test your design! See how it performs in the wild (aka real life) across different devices: tiny phones or giant desktop screens alike! Gather feedback from real users & make adjustments accordingly—you wouldn't want something that works great for one device but struggles with another!

So remember: keep things simple; make them fast & easy-peasy to use! Ensure your design looks fab on all screens while avoiding annoying distractions plus always consider accessibility too! Your ultimate goal? Craft an experience so smooth & enjoyable that users can browse on their phones in bed or work happily away on their laptops without any headaches!

"Step one of every project: Panic. Step two: Pretend to know what you're doing. Step three: Design something awesome."

Selecting typography, Moodboard & Color palette

Alrighty then! When you're getting into typography, moodboards, & color palettes, that's where the magic—err, I mean, design—begins to shape up. It's all about your project, the right vibes and making sure the visuals match the feelings you want for your website or app. Let's dive into this, shall we?

Typography (aka those fancy fonts)

Choosing the right fonts is a bit like picking an outfit for a party. You wouldn't show up in a tux at a beach bash, would ya? Nope! Same goes for fonts. You gotta find one that vibes with the personality of your brand or project.

For something all serious biz, think clean & simple—like sans-serif fonts. Yeah, go for minimalism; Helvetica or Arial are good pals here.

On the other hand, if you're leaning towards something fun and quirky? Well, then you can let loose with some flashy fonts (but not too much—just 2 or 3 max). Otherwise, it'll look like a font explosion!

The main thing? Keep it readable! You want the text to jump out and say "Hi!" on every possible device—especially mobiles since they're like everyone's best buddy these days.

Moodboard

Now, let's chat about moodboards. Think of it as your design's vibe check (yes, I said vibe). This is where you collect inspiration & ideas—like collecting Pokémon cards but way cooler! Gather images, colors, fonts—even textures—that give off the right energy for your project.

Picture curating an Instagram feed that's just screaming style: whether it's sleek & modern or bold & colorful or chill & minimalist. It helps you and anyone involved get in sync before diving into real designing because no one wants to design in chaos!

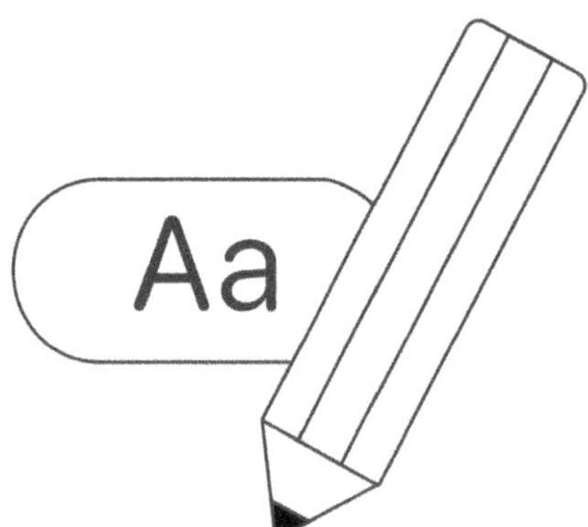

Color palette

Next up—the color palette! This is where you really nail down the look. You're picking colors that will carry through every inch of the design. You want them to match up nicely & play well together.

- First off: choose a few base colors (the main ones for backgrounds, headers—you know the drill), plus some fun accent colors to make certain things pop—like call-to-action buttons saying "Click me!"
- Colors totally set moods: blues feel calm (like that one friend who never freaks out), reds are energetic (perfect for morning people), greens are fresh (hello nature!), etc.

But hold on! Too many colors? Yikes! You'll be swimming in chaos. Stick with one main color, a secondary buddy color, and maybe one or two accent hues. Think cohesive design—not like someone dumped a box of crayons all over your work!

Oh! And don't forget about color contrasts. Make sure there's enough difference between background shades and text so that it's easy-peasy to read. Plus consider everyone—some folks might be colorblind; testing your palette is vital!

So there you have it: typography, moodboards, and color palettes are basically your trusty toolkit to create that overall vibe for your site or app. Get these things down right—and boom—the design will be chef's kiss!

High-fidelity designs (Finished design)

Okay, let's dive into the world of high-fidelity designs (or high-fi for short). Think of it as the final, shiny version of your project. This is the big moment when everything comes together and looks just like it will in real life! Picture a website or app that's practically begging to be launched tomorrow. It's dressed to impress—no more placeholders or sketchy doodles. Everything now sparkles with style!

Here's how it goes: In the early days, you were dealing with low-fidelity wireframes. Those were like rough drafts—kinda messy and basic. You just jotted down where stuff would eventually go. Fast forward to high-fi. Now, you're throwing in the real colors, fancy fonts, images, and content that show everyone what you really meant. Every button, link, and image grabs its place nicely. It looks clean and ready for action!

So what makes it high-fi?

- Detailed Visuals: You're finally working with all the cool stuff! Your brand colors are in full force, your typography is on lockdown, and your images? High quality all the way. It's like you went from a funky doodle to a stunning magazine cover.
- Real Content: Say goodbye to "Lorem ipsum" gibberish and those boring placeholder images! You've got actual text and genuine pics or videos ready for the spotlight. It's like switching out a plastic mannequin for a real model strutting down the runway!
- Interaction Design: Now you're thinking about how folks will use your design. Buttons that change color when hovered over? Check! Functional dropdown menus? You bet! All those slick animations are ready to play too. If someone clicks something, they'll get feedback! No awkward silence here; think of it as a mini celebration every time they interact.
- Pixel-Perfect: Every pixel is in its rightful place. You obsess over spacing, alignment, & proportions—making sure everything looks just right. Imagine a tailor checking every stitch so there are no goofy hiccups—it should be perfect!
- Usability Tested: By this stage, you've already pondered user experience (UX) like a wise sage and ironed out most problems! Now you're testing to ensure that not only do things look fab but they also work smoothly too! It should be simple to navigate on any gadget—mobile or desktop—and users should feel like pros without scratching their heads!
- Interactive Prototypes: Sometimes these high-fi designs get turned into prototypes! That means people can click through them as if they're using the actual app or website! Sure, it's not live code yet—but it feels so real that users might start planning their next adventure right there!

Now let's talk about why high-fi designs are super important.

- High-fidelity designs are like your grand finale presentation to clients or stakeholders ready for applause! It has to look sharp because this is what they'll expect when the website or app finally hits the internet runway. It's like bringing your science project to class—everyone will judge how well you put it together!
- But there's more! Developers adore these polished designs too. Unlike low-fi sketches that leave everything up for grabs, high-fi gives them all the precise details they need. They get an exact blueprint making their coding adventures easier because they know exactly what they're building!
- In a nutshell, high-fi designs are your glorious creations ready for prime time. You've taken all those brainstorming sessions and rough sketches & turned them into an interactive masterpiece that folks will actually use! This is when your vision struts onto center stage—all crisp and professional—but with a wink and some

humor thrown in for good measure!

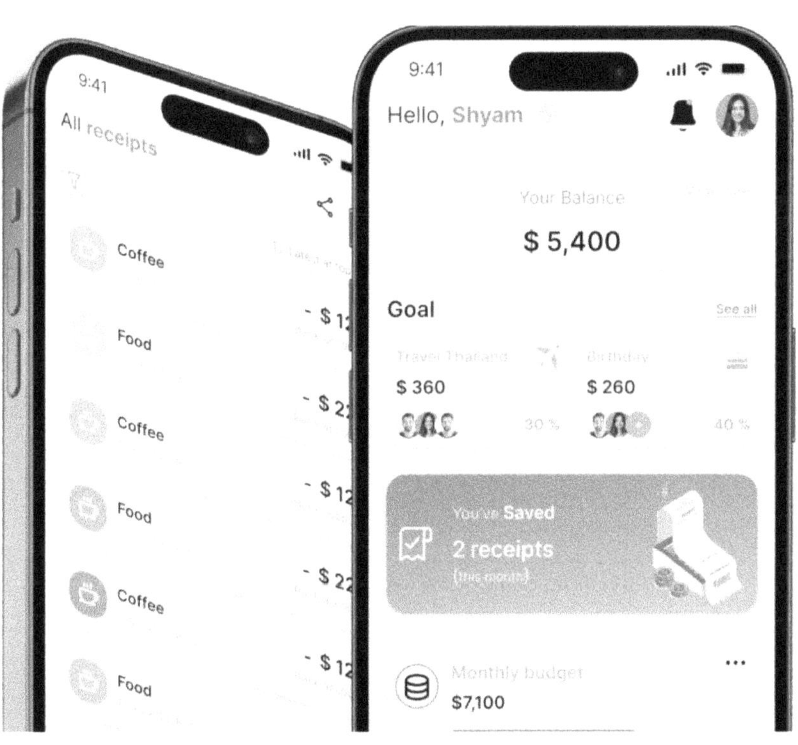

40

Interactive design and prototyping

Interactive design & prototyping is where your designs go from boring old pictures to fun, clickable apps or websites. It's not just about looking pretty anymore—it's about making them work like users want.

Interactive Design

Interactive design is all about how folks mess with your app or site. Picture this: every button click, swipe, and hover should feel smooth as butter. You want users to flow through it without scratching their heads about what comes next—it should feel totally natural.

Think of Instagram: you tap a photo to give it a thumbs up, swipe through stories like you're on a rollercoaster, or pull down to refresh your feed. All these actions? Yep, that's interactive design strutting its stuff! You make sure the app reacts to every tiny user action in a way that makes them go, "Wow, this is easy-peasy!"

So, when someone clicks a button, does it throw a little color party? Does a menu slide out like it's doing the cha-cha when they hit that hamburger icon? Interactive design nails those tiny moments that keep users interested & happy.

Prototyping

Next up, prototyping! This is where you grab your interactive design ideas and put them to the test—like a dress rehearsal for your app but without the fancy coding. You whip up a clickable version of your design so users can poke around—this way, they can get the vibe of how the final product is gonna be before you've even built it.

Think of a prototype as a pretend version of your app or website where users can press buttons, click links & explore menus—even if everything isn't shiny & finished yet. You can show these prototypes off to clients or teammates and gather their two cents before diving into real development.

For instance, if you're working on a shopping app, your prototype might allow users to scroll through products, add items to their cart like pros, and peek at the checkout page—without any back-end voodoo needed. You're just faking the experience so people can see how it'll work & look.

Why Prototyping is Key

Prototyping is super important because it lets you spot any goofy design quirks or confusing bits before diving too deep into development land. You can play around with different interactions and see what flows smoothly. Plus! It's an awesome way to let clients or stakeholders mess around with it early on—hands-on feedback time!

It's kind of like building a LEGO model of a house before actually putting in drywall—you want all doors, windows & rooms in tip-top order before committing to the big build.

In short: interactive design is all about getting users involved with your creation, and prototyping? That's turning those ideas into something they can actually push & poke at! It's like taking flat art and turning it into a video game where they can tap, swipe & have fun before it's fully baked!

CHAPTER SEVEN

HANDING OVER YOUR DESIGN

Review your design and be ready for client revisions

Alright, so after all that hard work and your design looking absolutely awesome, take a minute—just one—to step back. Look at it with fresh eyes. This is a big moment! You wanna make sure it's all great before your client lays eyes on it. Because, oh boy, they are gonna have feedback—get ready!

When reviewing your design, you've got to think like a user.

Ask yourself:

Is the flow nice & smooth? Is everything easy to find? Does it make any sense at all? Also, watch out for tiny mistakes. You know, things like text that's not lined up right, odd spaces that throw off the vibe, or links that go nowhere. You need to catch these little gremlins before the client spots them. It's gotta look sharp and ready for the spotlight!

Now here's the kicker:

Be prepared for client changes. No matter how much blood, sweat, and tears you put into it, clients often want adjustments. Maybe they'll say "Oops! That color is soooo last season." Or they might want to move things around like they're playing Tetris with your design. Just remember - it's not personal! It's all part of the fun.

Think about it this way:

Client feedback is like a dance. It's not criticism; it's a collaboration where you both just want to create something that rocks for their business and users. So when they come back with requests, just go with the flow! Make the changes, share your thoughts if needed (but not too much), and keep rolling along.

In short: review it, fix what needs fixing & then get ready to make those client tweaks like a total pro. You got this!

Usability testing

Usability testing is like the ultimate vibe check for your design. You could call it the "Is this even usable?" moment. You've spent a ton of time—like, hours—getting the layout just right choosing pretty fonts & making everything look pixel-perfect. But here's the kicker: now you need to see if real, live humans can actually use it without feeling like they've wandered into a maze!

Picture this:

you hand someone your phone and say, "Hey, give this a whirl!" Then, you watch them interact with your app or website. It's kind of like watching a cat with a laser pointer. You're checking to see if they get stuck at any point, if anything confuses them, or if they take forever to do something that should be as easy as pie.

During the usability test, users have some tasks to do—like finding a product (easy-peasy), filling out a form (not too bad), or wandering around the site (make sure they don't get lost in the Bermuda Triangle!). And you? Well, you just sit back and observe. The whole mission is to catch any head-scratchers that you might have missed because you're too close to the project (like really close). Let's face it: what makes perfect sense to you might totally make someone else's head spin.

Oh, and you're not there to explain anything! Nope! Just let them explore like they're on an adventurous treasure hunt—except instead of gold coins, they're just looking for a nice pair of shoes. If they struggle, that's your cue: something needs some serious fixing! Maybe those buttons are hiding better than a shy kid at a school dance or your navigation is sneakier than a cat at midnight.

So, what's the main takeaway?

Usability testing is all about finding out if your design actually works for people out there in the wild. It's all about making sure everything's super easy to use & doesn't make anyone want to pull their hair out!

CHAPTER EIGHT

DON'T WORRY YOU'LL LEARN GRADUALLY AS THE JOURNEY CONTINUES

Take a deep breath

No need to freak out if things didn't snap into place super fast. UX design is a wild ride kind of like a rollercoaster and you don't become a pro in one night. It's like trying to learn to skate—you might take a tumble or two (or three), but guess what? Each time you get back, you're totally cooler than before!

Just keep pushing yourself.

Keep trying new stuff! As you dive into projects, things will start to click—like when you finally find the right way to untangle those pesky headphones.

Skills will land in your lap, shortcuts will pop up like daisies in spring, & you'll discover what works best for YOU. No need to race, my friend—everyone's got their own speed.

After tackling just a few projects, you'll look back and think, "Wow, I've really leveled up!" So trust the journey & have fun along the way! It's all part of the adventure!

"UX design is 90% Googling how to do stuff and 10% pretending you knew it all along."

9 789889 588083